Villains

SUZANNE MUIR

Editorial Board
David Booth • Joan Green • Jack Booth

STECK-VAUGHN
Harcourt Achieve

www.HarcourtAchieve.com

10801 N. Mopac Expressway
Building # 3
Austin, TX 78759
1.800.531.5015

Steck-Vaughn is a trademark of Harcourt Achieve Inc. registered in the
United States of America and/or other jurisdictions. All inquiries should
be mailed to Harcourt Achieve Inc., P.O. Box 27010, Austin, TX 78755.

Ru'bĭcon © 2006 Rubicon Publishing Inc.
www.rubiconpublishing.com

Project Editors: Miriam Bardswich, Kim Koh
Editorial Assistant: Lori McNeelands
Art/Creative Director: Jennifer Drew-Tremblay
Assistant Art Director: Jen Harvey
Designer: Jan-John Rivera

6 7 8 9 10   5 4 3 2 1

Villains
ISBN 1-41902-389-6

CONTENTS

WATCH
OUT!

VILLAINS
AT LARGE

...

300 a.d

600 a.d

900 a.d

300

The villain is the evil person in a story.

The word villain comes from the Latin word "villa," which means "someone who lived in a village."

In the Middle Ages, rich and powerful people believed that villagers were not important. They called them "villains." That's why many villains are portrayed as being old, poor, or dirty.

Whether the villain is evil like Green Goblin or silly like Floop from *Spy Kids*, villains make a story exciting.

portrayed: *shown*

COMMON TYPES OF VILLAINS

Pirates	Witches
Monsters	Creatures
Prisoners	Evil Scientists
Crooks	Burglars
Tricksters	Robbers
Murderers	Ogres
Kidnappers	Bullies

wrap up

In a group, think of five characteristics of a villain. As you read, compare your list with the villains in this book.

VILLAINS
WANTED

$50.00 REWARD
HAVE YOU SEEN THIS GORGON?

Description:
- Female gorgon
- Instead of hair, Medusa's head is covered with slithering snakes.
- Burning red eyes

Last Seen: Living in a cave just outside of city limits.

Be advised that Medusa is extremely dangerous. Do not approach this woman — one look from her could turn you to stone!

gorgon: *half human being and half beast*

ALL!

WANTED

$50.00 REWARD FOR THE CAPTURE OF THE TROLL

Description:
- Ugly, ugly, ugly!
- Large ears
- Big nose
- Large teeth
- Usually wears clothes made of animal skins

Guilty Of: Attempted murder of three billy goats.

Most Likely Seen: Under a bridge

Although not known as a danger to humans, the Troll is capable of anything. (Come on! He tried

ESCAPED

THE BIG BAD WOLF

Description:
- Covered in brown fur
- Seriously needs a bath and brushing
- Terrible breath

Favorite Food: Plump little pigs

Guilty Of: Destroying personal property and frightening three little pigs.

Most Likely Seen: Lurking around farms.

If you spot the Big Bad Wolf, call the police immediately! The wolf is very fast and very violent — do not try and capture the wolf on your own.

Lurking: *creeping about*

HAVE YOU SEEN THIS EVIL QUEEN?

$150.00 REWARD

Description:
- Black hair
- Red lips
- Evil green eyes
- Fair skin

Last Seen: Talking to a magic mirror.

Guilty Of: Attempted murder by poisoned apple.

The Queen is a dangerous repeat offender. She is very jealous, especially of those she thinks are prettier than her.

wrap up

Do you know which story each villain comes from? Write a newspaper report about one of the villains and his/her crime.

Captain
MIDNIGHT

Paper texture–istockphoto; illustrations by Luke Markle

warm up

This story is based on characters from *Peter Pan* by J.M. Barrie. If you have read the book or seen the movie, share what you know.

In a faraway place there lived a wicked pirate. He was the meanest, greediest man on the seas. His name was Captain Hook.

Captain Hook had only one goal in life — and that was to get rid of Peter Pan, the leader of the Lost Boys.

One day Captain Hook stood on his ship peering through the telescope towards a small island.

"Arggggh," he grunted. "I have to catch that silly little Peter Pan and his fairy Tinkerbell. Then I would be able to find all the treasure in the world — without him stopping me!"

Just then Captain Hook spotted Peter Pan and his gang of Lost Boys. They were talking to a little girl and her brothers. Captain Hook strained to hear their conversation.

Hook's SNACK

"Oh Peter Pan," said the girl. "Neverland is more beautiful than I had imagined."

"Wendy, just wait until we show you the treasure. You won't believe your eyes!" exclaimed Peter Pan with a laugh.

Captain Hook smiled a wicked grin. He began plotting how he would capture Peter Pan.

"I will kidnap the girl and her brothers. Then Peter Pan will have to rescue them. When he comes to my ship — Snap! I will feed him to Croc. Ha, ha, ha!"

plotting: *planning*

Captain Hook put his plan into action. He kidnapped Wendy and her brothers. Then he left a note for Peter Pan to come and rescue them. Now all he had to do was wait.

"You let us go, you mean pirate!" yelled Wendy at Captain Hook.

"Zip it, little girl or I'll feed you to Croc. He hasn't eaten anything all week so he's **v-e-r-y** hungry!" sneered Captain Hook.

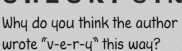

CHECKPOINT

Why do you think the author wrote "v-e-r-y" this way?

At that moment, Peter slipped on some water and crashed into a box of empty glass jars. They fell to the ground with a loud crash! Captain Hook jumped out of bed. The other pirates rushed out. They surrounded Wendy, Michael, John, and Peter Pan.

"Ah ha! Look at this, boys. Our friend Peter Pan has joined us for a little midnight snack. Too bad **he's the snack**," laughed Captain Hook.

CHECKPOINT

What do you think this means?

There was a loud "tick! tock!" Croc jumped up from the water snapping his sharp teeth in delight. Quickly, the pirates tied up Peter Pan and the children. Then they lined them up to walk the plank.

Tinkerbell flew up and down trying to think of a way to save them.

Out of the corner of her eye, Tinkerbell saw a box of bananas. She had a great idea. She sprinkled fairy dust over the box. At once, the bananas spilled all over the ship's

"Don't worry, Peter Pan will come and save us," said Wendy to her brothers.

"Oh yes, that's exactly what he'll do," smiled Captain Hook.

That night while Captain Hook was sleeping, Wendy heard the sound of bells ringing in her ear. Rubbing her eyes, she woke up and saw Peter Pan standing in front of her. A little fairy was fluttering behind him.

"Oh Peter! I knew you would come for us," whispered a happy Wendy.

"Tinkerbell led me here," said Peter. "Come on now, there's no time. Captain Hook could wake up at any moment."

CHECKPOINT

Notice that the author uses a lot of dialogue in this story. Why do you think the author has done this?

deck. As the pirates rushed to push the children toward the plank, they stepped on the bananas … one by one, they slipped and slid right over the edge of the ship.

"Whoa, what the …?" screamed Captain Hook as he slid past Peter and Wendy.

Mean old Captain Hook landed right in the water!

"Quickly Tinkerbell, undo the ropes," shouted Peter. Tinkerbell freed the children and Peter. She sprinkled fairy dust over them.

They all flew off the ship!

Down below in the water, Captain Hook and his pirates were madly swimming to escape Croc (who was snapping his huge jaws after them).

"This is not the end, Peter Pan! I'll get you yet or my name isn't Captain Hook!" shouted the pirate as Croc chased him out into the ocean.

"Here you go, Hook," Peter Pan chuckled. He tossed Hook a banana. "It looks like Croc is getting his midnight snack after all."

wrap up

List three things about Captain Hook that indicates he's a villain.

THE

With a partner, practice reading this poem aloud. Be sure to make it dramatic.

WENDIGO

By Ogden Nash

The Wendigo,
The Wendigo!
Its eyes are ice and indigo!
Its blood is rank and yellowish!
Its voice is hoarse and bellowish!
Its tentacles are slithery,
And scummy,
Slimy,
Leathery!
Its lips are hungry, blubbery,
And smacky,
Sucky,
Rubbery!

The Wendigo,
The Wendigo!
I saw it just a friend ago!
Last night it lurked in Canada;
Tonight, on your veranda!
As you are lolling hammockwise
It contemplates you stomachwise.
You loll,
It contemplates,
It lollops.
The rest is merely gulps and gollops.

lurked: *crept about*
contemplates: *thinks about*

CHECKPOINT
Think about it! What do you think has happened to the friend?

wrap up

Create a "wanted poster" for the Wendigo. Draw a picture of the creature. Write a short description of what it does. Offer a reward for its capture. (Turn to page 8 for an example.)

WENDIGO'S CHILDREN

Illustrated by MIKE ROOTH

LONG AGO, THE FIRST PEOPLES KNEW OF A DANGEROUS CREATURE CALLED A "WENDIGO." IT WOULD LURE BOYS AND GIRLS OUT OF THEIR BEDS INTO THE DEEP FORESTS. ONCE THE WENDIGO HAD ITS VICTIM, IT WOULD SINK ITS TEETH INTO THEM AND DRAIN OUT ALL OF THEIR BLOOD.

SO THEY'RE KINDA LIKE VAMPIRES?

YES.

WHEN THE WENDIGO MOVED INTO AN AREA, THE PEOPLE MOVED AWAY. BUT THIS TIME THEY HAD FOUND A BEAUTIFUL PLACE TO LIVE WITH PLENTY OF HUNTING AND FISHING.

SO THE PEOPLE DECIDED TO KILL THE WENDIGO.

THEY DUG A VERY DEEP PIT, AND PLACED BRANCHES AND LEAVES TO HIDE IT.

THEN THE MOST BEAUTIFUL GIRL AND THE STRONGEST YOUNG MAN LAY DOWN NEAR THE PIT AND PRETENDED TO SLEEP.

SOON THE WENDIGO CAME TO CAPTURE THEM BUT AS SOON AS HE STEPPED ON THE BRANCHES, HE FELL INTO THE PIT.

AAHIIIIIIEEEEE

ALL THE PEOPLE CAME RUNNING AND THREW BURNING LOGS INTO THE PIT. SOON THE ENTIRE PIT WAS ON FIRE.

SUDDENLY THERE WAS A HUGE EXPLOSION. SMOKE AND ASHES WERE THROWN INTO THE AIR.

YOU MAY HAVE KILLED ME, BUT I WILL HAVE FINAL REVENGE! MY CHILDREN WILL SUCK THE BLOOD OF YOUR CHILDREN FOREVER!

THE ASHES TURNED INTO MOSQUITOES AND STARTED TO BITE THE PEOPLE. AND THEY HAVE DONE SO EVER SINCE.

OUCH! I THINK ANOTHER WENDIGO JUST BIT ME!

HA HA! WE NEED SOME MORE WENDIGO SPRAY!

wrap up

1. Wendigo stories vary among different groups of American Indians. Write your own short story about the origin of mosquitoes.

2. With a friend, discuss how the story of the Wendigo is similar to the story of vampires.

What Type of Hero Are You?

1. If you had to save someone from a villain, would you:

a) Call the police for help?
b) Try to confuse the villain so the prisoner could sneak away?
c) Dash in, grab the person, and rush out?

2. If you could have a magic item to help you defeat villains, you would have:

a) A genie who could keep the villain busy while you get help.
b) A magic harp that puts villains to sleep.
c) No need for help. I could defeat a villain on my own.

3. If you knew that a troll lived under the bridge on your walk to school, would you:

a) Go another way?
b) Tiptoe very lightly and try to sneak across the bridge?
c) March bravely across the bridge.

4. To punish a villain who has been caught, you would:

a) Leave it up to the police. They can lock up the villain.
b) Give the villain a book about good behavior.
c) Keep the villain in your house to do your chores. You can handle him/her!

Find out about your heroic self on page 48!

The Real Dracula

warm up

Have you ever seen a movie about vampires? Was it scary? Share your stories in a small group.

Was Dracula a real person? Or was he created by an imaginative author? Dracula, the evil vampire of tales and movies, was a combination of the two.

FYI

The name Dracula means "son of the Dragon" — probably because there was a picture of a dragon on his family's crest.

Did you know that bloodsucking bats actually exist? That's right — in Mexico and South America there are bats that feed on blood. This is one of the reasons that bats are linked to vampires.

Some people think that Dracula was based on the bloodthirsty Prince Vlad.

The real Dracula was someone known as Prince Vlad, who was born in Romania during the early 1400s. After his father was murdered, Prince Vlad became the ruler of Wallachia. Once in power, he avenged his father's death by killing all his enemies. Several thousands of people were put to death during this time. But Prince Vlad didn't just kill people — he tortured them!

Some people think that Dracula, the famous vampire in Bram Stoker's book, *Dracula*, was based on the bloodthirsty Prince Vlad.

Over the years, storytellers have given vampires like Dracula certain character traits.

---

avenged: *to get revenge*

Some stories tell of vampires who suck blood and change into bats, wolves, and even mist.

In the past, people protected themselves from these bloodsucking beasts by hanging cloves of garlic around their homes. This tradition is described in Bram Stoker's *Dracula*:

"We went into the room, taking the flowers with us. First the Professor fastened up the windows and latched them securely; next, taking a handful, he rubbed them all over the sashes, as though to ensure that every whiff of air that might get in would be laden with the garlic smell. Then with the wisp he rubbed all over the jamb of the door, above, below, and at each side, and round the fireplace in the same way …

"We then waited whilst Lucy made her toilet for the night, and when she was in bed he came and himself fixed the wreath of garlic round her neck. The last words he said to her were, "Take care you do not disturb it; and even if the room feels close, do not tonight open the window or the door."

laden: *covered*
wisp: *small bunch*
jamb: *frame*

CHECKPOINT
Notice how people protected themselves from Dracula.

wrap up

1. Why do you think people in the past used garlic to protect themselves from Dracula?

2. If you ever met Dracula, how would you defend yourself? Write your plan in three steps.

WEB CONNECTIONS

Using the Internet, find out more symbols associated with vampires. Draw a picture and provide a description for each symbol.

TOP 5 SIGNS YOUR NEIGHBOR MAY BE A VERY VILE VILLAIN!

1 They refer to themselves in the third person.

AH, DIRT... THE ETERNAL FOE! I SEE YOU TREMBLE WITH FEAR IN THE FACE OF THE CLEANING GIANT! WHO SHALL WIN THIS BATTLE?

2 They laugh too deep and too long at things only they find funny.

FOOL! THERE IS NO "BRENDA" HERE! YOU HAVE ONCE AGAIN FAILED AT DIALING THE CORRECT NUMBER SEQUENCE!

BWAA-HA-HA-HA-HA-HA-HA!

3 They say things like "vengeance will be mine"...

I WILL BIDE MY TIME ... AND WHEN THE TIME IS RIPE AND THE HANDS OF FATE POINT IN MY FAVOR, I SHALL WEED YOU ALL ...

AND VENGEANCE WILL BE MINE!

4 They keep henchmen around the house.

THE MACARONI WAS DELICIOUS YET AGAIN, NUMBER 5! NOW FETCH ME MY DEATH RAY! CHOP CHOP!

5 Their house is actually a secret hideout.

HOW DID YOU FIND ME? WHO SENT YOU?

UH, I'M HERE TO HOOK UP YOUR CABLE ... ?

RELEASE THE HOUNDS!!!

vengeance: *revenge*

Hodja and the Thief

Retold by Suzanne Muir

warm up

Hodja is a Middle Eastern wise man/trickster. Can you name some other storybook character who is both good and bad?

Once upon a time in a Middle Eastern land, there lived a very wise man named Hodja. Hodja spent his time riding backwards on his donkey, going from village to village helping people with their problems.

One evening, Hodja returned to his home after a long day's journey. He was very tired and ready for a good rest. Just before he went to bed, he stopped to admire his new carpet. It was a brilliant shade of red and had a very special pattern. Hodja was so busy enjoying his beautiful carpet that he forgot to shut the window when he went to bed.

In the middle of the night, a thief slipped into Hodja's room.

"Ah Hodja, I will take this carpet and enjoy it in my own home," whispered the thief. He rolled up the carpet. The noise woke up Hodja. He opened one eye and watched the thief. Instead of trying to save his carpet, Hodja shrugged his shoulders and kept very still. The thief lifted the carpet onto his shoulders, and climbed out the window.

The next morning, Hodja ate a big breakfast. Then he gathered some belongings and went to the thief's home. He knocked on the door. When the thief opened the door and saw Hodja, he was flustered. His cheeks became as red as the carpet.

flustered: *nervous*

CHECKPOINT

Why do you think Hodja let the thief get away?

FYI

Hodja was a real man born in Turkey in 1208. That means his stories are more than 700 years old!

Hodja did not say a word. He simply dropped off his things. Then he went back home and gathered some more belongings. He dropped them off at the thief's home as well. Back and forth Hodja went all morning, silently dropping off his clothes, his furniture, and his dishes at the thief's door.

The thief grew more and more confused. Finally, he could not take it anymore. He stopped Hodja and asked, "Hodja why do you bring me all your worldly belongings?"

Hodja smiled and replied, "My friend, last night when you came to my house and took my carpet, I thought you wanted me to come and live with you but were too shy to ask me. So, I'm moving in today!"

CHECKPOINT
Notice how Hodja shows the thief that he has done something wrong.

The thief helped Hodja carry all his belongings back home, including the beautiful red carpet. He never bothered Hodja again.

wrap up

1. Look at the illustrations for this story. List three things about Hodja's home that are different from yours.

2. In the voice of the thief, write a short letter to Hodja apologizing for stealing his carpet.

WEB CONNECTIONS

Using the Internet, type **"Hodja"** into a search engine. Find out about the countries that Hodja stories come from, such as Turkey or Egypt. Share your findings with the class.

Doctor Octopus

Spider-Man's Arch-enemy

Originally, Doctor Octopus was a brilliant scientist. He was so clever that he designed robotic arms to help him in his atomic research. During a freak accident, the robotic arms were attached to his body. The accident also affected his mind. Doctor Octopus was **transformed** into a criminal mastermind.

warm up

Think about your favorite villain. Has a movie been created with this villain in it?

transformed: *changed, made into something else*

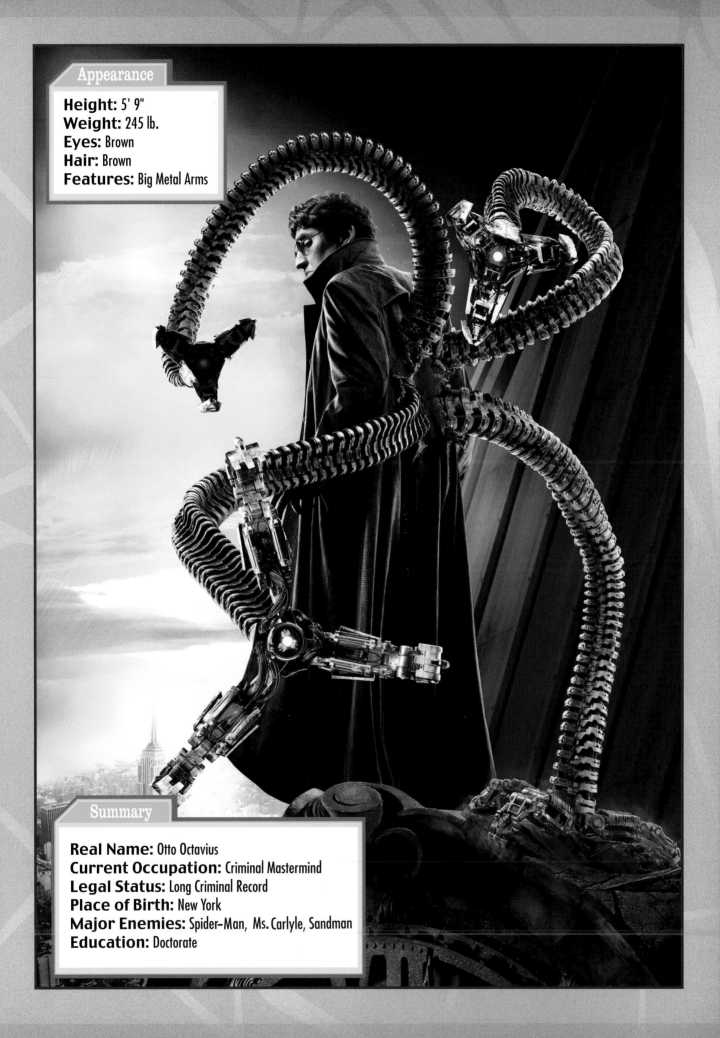

Appearance

Height: 5' 9"
Weight: 245 lb.
Eyes: Brown
Hair: Brown
Features: Big Metal Arms

Summary

Real Name: Otto Octavius
Current Occupation: Criminal Mastermind
Legal Status: Long Criminal Record
Place of Birth: New York
Major Enemies: Spider-Man, Ms. Carlyle, Sandman
Education: Doctorate

Alfred Molina played Doctor Octopus in the movie *Spider-Man 2*. In this interview, Paul Fisher talks with Alfred Molina about the role.

Paul Fisher: What was strange about wearing that costume and, as an actor, how tough is it?

Alfred Molina: Well, it's only tough in the sense that it is constricting but what you have to do is kind of find a way of dealing with it. I very quickly discovered that I couldn't bend and turn and shift my weight and twist in quite the same way.

P.F.: Well, what about interacting with the puppeteer arms?

A.M.: Well, we had a fantastic team of puppeteers, about 16 to 15 guys and one woman and a wonderful choreographer.

CHECKPOINT ⬆

What do you think a choreographer is?

The puppeteers and myself worked together very closely … So we could do great big things, like push a hole through a building, but at the same time do delicate things like taking off a pair of glasses.

P.F.: How long did it take to put on and take off [the costume and makeup]?

A.M.: Well, the whole thing from suit to nuts, like including all the make-up and everything was probably about two, two and a half hours.

---

tough: *difficult*
constricting: *difficult to move*

…: *These dots are called an "ellipsis." They are used when text has been left out of a piece of writing.*

P.F.: Did you read the Marvel comics as a kid? Or were you familiar with Doc Oc already?

A.M.: Yes to the first question, no to the second one. I did read them when I was a kid and I collected them a little bit.

P.F.: Which ones?

A.M.: Marvel comics.

P.F.: Just any of them?

A.M.: Yeah, whatever I could get my hands on. I don't remember reading any Doc Oc stories at that time. I don't remember him as a character when I was actively reading.

P.F.: Did you look at any of the books?

A.M.: Yeah I went back and checked them out. I was curious to see how he was drawn because he changed. I think Doc Oc first appeared in the mid-60s and depending on who was drawing him, he changed. He went through various changes but the one thing that stayed constant was this wonderful, almost cruel sense of humor ... I thought that was the really interesting quality.

P.F.: Are you prepared for the comic book fans coming up to you?

A.M.: They already are, they come to the stage door at the theater in New York and you know, it's great.

P.F.: How interested would you be if Sam [the Director] called you and asked you to come back and do a cameo in *Spider-Man 3*?

Molina: I would be very happy.

_____

cameo: *a small part*

wrap up

Imagine Spider-Man and Doctor Octopus standing face to face on an empty street. What happens? Draw four frames of a comic strip to tell the story.

WEB CONNECTIONS

Use the Internet to find images of Doctor Octopus. In groups of three, find out how Doctor Octopus' appearance and personality has changed over the years. Use a character organizer to record this information.

Very Villainous Fun

What is a giant's favorite snack?

A big mac truck.

Villainous Quotes

Can you match these famous villains to their famous sayings?

The Wicked Witch of the West	"Off with her head!"
	"Riddle me this, riddle me that. Who's afraid of the big black bat?"
Evil Queen	
	"Walk the plank!"
Cruella DeVil	
	"All the better to eat you with, my dear."
Queen of Hearts	
	"I'll get you my pretty, and your little dog too!"
Captain Hook	
	"Don't underestimate the power of the dark side."
The Riddler	
	"Mirror, mirror on the wall, who's the fairest of them all?"
The Wolf	
	"Ah my only true love, darling ... furs. I live for furs. I worship furs!"
Darth Vader	

Giant
Sea Witch
Darth Vader
Joker
Grinch
Troll
Wicked Witch
Green Goblin
Queen
Captain Hook
Cruella DeVil

Across

1. He stole all the presents from the Whos in Who-ville.

2. She always wears a black and white fur coat. Most dogs hate her.

3. "By hook or by crook I'll get Peter Pan by the end of this book."

4. He lives under the bridge that the three billy goats crossed.

5. Dorothy and her dog Toto must escape her evil clutches.

6. Snow White ate her poisoned apple.

Down

1. A green masked man who ruins Spider-Man's plans.

7. Batman doesn't think his jokes are funny.

8. Jack steals his magic hen who lays the golden eggs.

9. The evil one who took away the Little Mermaid's voice.

10. He wears a black helmet and is Luke's father.

Answers on page 48

Why did the witch buy a new spoon?
To stir things up.

warm up

Have you ever listened to a story being told? Read this story as if you were a storyteller. Be sure to change the sound of your voice to match the different characters.

THE GREAT RAJAH LION

By Hezekiah Butterworth from his book
Zig Zag Journey in India (1887)

Illustrations by Jan-John Rivera

The Great Rajah Lion. He used to ro-ar, — ro-ar so loud that the little animals of the forest would fall down dead and he would eat them. That was the way he hunted.

The lion roared until he had killed and eaten all the animals in the jungle except two little jackals. These were two cunning little jackals.

A hard time of it they had. They ran hither and thither, and tried to keep beyond the sound of the lion's voice, which had been death to all other animals. One was a Husband Jackal, and the other a Wife Jackal.

Every day the little Wife Jackal would say, "Husband, Husband, I am afraid he will catch us today."

Then they would hear the lion roar, far away, like thunder.

"Never fear, little wife," the Husband Jackal would say, "my wit will save you."

CHECKPOINT
What do you think he means?

"Let us run," the Wife Jackal would then say, "quick, quick!"

"Quick, quick!" said the Husband Jackal, always.

Then the two would run quick, quick, out of the hearing of the voice of the lion.

Rajah: *Indian king*
jackals: *wild dogs*
hither and thither: *here and there*

But one day, when they thought the lion had left the jungle, they chanced to run right before the lion's eyes as he was returning home.

"Oh, Husband, Husband, what shall we do?"

"Be quiet, and trust me; wit will save us."

"Let us run quick, quick, before he roars, little Wife, — quick, quick, right towards his den!"

CHECKPOINT
Does this surprise you?

So the two cunning little jackals ran quick, quick, towards the lion's den.

The lion was much astonished, and forgot to roar.

"Quick, quick, little Husband!"

"Quick, quick, little Wife, into the lion's den."

The lion came home after them.

"Now, you little wretches, I have got you and will eat you. Come here, for I am hungry," growled the lion.

"Oh, Rajah Lion, listen! We know that you are our master; but there is a Rajah in the jungle that is greater than you."

"Greater, greater? There is no monarch of the jungle but me."

"Oh, Rajah, Rajah, come with us and see. We will show him to you, for we know where he can be seen."

"Show me the Rajah, and I will save you and destroy him. I will be king alone."

---

astonished: *surprised*

monarch: *ruler*

The little jackals ran out of the den, followed by the lion. They came to a deep pool in the middle of the rocks.

And the full moon was shining.

"There he is," said the Husband Jackal. "Quick, quick!"

"There he is," said the Wife Jackal. "Quick, quick!"

"Look, look!" said both.

The lion shook his mane, and looked over the cliff. He thought that he saw another lion in a den below.

"Don't roar," said the Husband Jackal.

"Don't roar," said the Wife Jackal.

The lion's eyes blazed. He looked again, and he shook his head. The other lion shook his head. The lion's heart was now on fire, and he leaped into the pool.

There was a splash and a gurgle; the moonbeams were broken in the water, and circled round and round. Then all was still; the pool became a mirror again.

The full moon was shining, and the two cunning little jackals sang.

"Ao, ao,

Ring-a-ting, Ring-a-ting."

wrap up

1. The Husband Jackal says, "Wit will save us." Explain how he used his wit in this story.

2. In a group of four, role-play the story. Decide who will play which part. Practice and present your play to the class.

FOILED!

Some people think that villains always get away with bad deeds. Sometimes, though, real-life villains do get caught.

warm up

Can you think of a time when you were caught doing something wrong? How did you feel?

A Great Escape

A man was trying to avoid going to court for a crime he had committed. He decided to try and escape by mailing himself in a crate to a Caribbean island. He told his friend about the plan. Then he packed enough food and water for the trip, and set off.

His friend waited to hear from him. A few days later, he started to get worried. The friend phoned the police. When the criminal was found he was tired and starving. It seems the shipping date had been postponed to the next month! Good thing he had a friend looking out for him.

postponed: *moved to a later date*

CHECKPOINT

Why would he mail himself in a crate?

00:53 11104102

When You've Got To Go ...

One night a man was awakened by strange noises. Guessing it was a burglar, the man carefully crept towards the sound. Suddenly he heard the toilet flush. Opening the door to the washroom he found the thief washing his hands. Quickly the man shut and blocked the bathroom door. His wife called the police. That's one burglar who wished he had waited until he got home.

21:43 04110103

A Sticky Situation

A variety store clerk was shocked when two legs came out of the ceiling vent of his store. The thief was trying to break in through the ceiling so that he would not be seen. If he had measured first, he would have known that he was too big. He was stuck in the vent for five hours while police tried to get him out. When they did, he was arrested.

shocked: *surprised*

wrap up

1. Write a short newspaper report about one of these villains. Don't forget to create a catchy headline.

2. Pretend you are a superhero. What type of trap would you set to catch one of these villains? Build a model of your trap to share with the class.

The Walrus and the Carpenter

By Lewis Carroll, 1872

Excerpt from a poem in *Through the Looking Glass*

warm up

Have you ever been tricked into doing something? Read this poem and see who gets tricked and who gets a treat!

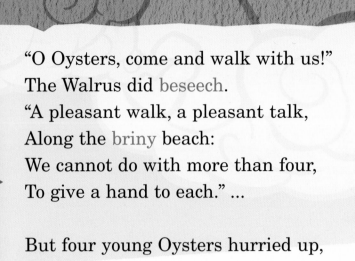

"O Oysters, come and walk with us!"
The Walrus did beseech.
"A pleasant walk, a pleasant talk,
Along the briny beach:
We cannot do with more than four,
To give a hand to each." ...

But four young Oysters hurried up,
All eager for the treat:
Their coats were brushed, their faces washed,
Their shoes were clean and neat —
And this was odd, because, you know,
They hadn't any feet.

---

beseech: *beg*
briny: *salty*

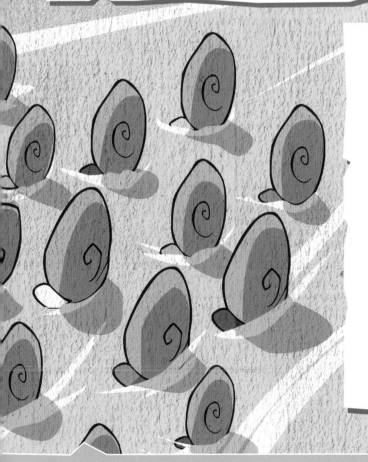

Four other Oysters followed them,
And yet another four;
And thick and fast they came at last,
And more, and more, and more —
All hopping through the frothy waves,
And scrambling to the shore.

The Walrus and the Carpenter
Walked on a mile or so,
And then they rested on a rock
Conveniently low:
And all the little Oysters stood
And waited in a row.

"The time has come," the Walrus said,
"To talk of many things:
Of shoes — and ships — and sealing-wax —
Of cabbages — and kings —
And why the sea is boiling hot —
And whether pigs have wings."

"But wait a bit," the Oysters cried,
"Before we have our chat;
For some of us are out of breath,
And all of us are fat!"
"No hurry!" said the Carpenter.
They thanked him much for that.

"A loaf of bread," the Walrus said,
"Is what we chiefly need:
Pepper and vinegar besides
Are very good indeed —
Now, if you're ready, Oysters dear,
We can begin to feed."

CHECKPOINT

What do you think the Walrus and
the Carpenter are going to do?

"But not on us!" the Oysters cried,
Turning a little blue.
"After such kindness, that would be
A dismal thing to do!"
"The night is fine," the Walrus said.
"Do you admire the view? ...

"It seems a shame," the Walrus said,
"To play them such a trick.
After we've brought them out so far,
And made them trot so quick!"
The Carpenter said nothing but
"The butter's spread too thick!"

"I weep for you," the Walrus said:
"I deeply sympathize."
With sobs and tears he sorted out
Those of the largest size,
Holding his pocket-handkerchief
Before his streaming eyes.

"O Oysters," said the Carpenter,
"You've had a pleasant run!
Shall we be trotting home again?"
But answer came there none —
And this was scarcely odd, because
They'd eaten every one.

CHECK POINT

Do you think the Walrus is really upset?

wrap up

1. In groups of three, read the poem out loud. Each person in the group can read a different role (Walrus, Carpenter, Oysters).

2. Pretend you are an oyster that escaped. Write a short note to your family telling them what happened to your friends.

What Type of Hero Are You? (from page 21)

Score 1 point for each 'a' answer that you chose. Score 2 points for every 'b' answer you picked, and score 3 points for each 'c' answer.

4-6: You are a sensible person who not only looks out for others, but yourself as well. You know that adults may be better able to deal with dangerous situations.

_____

sensible: *thinking things through*

7-10: You are a careful person. You are ready and willing to help out, but you don't rush into things — you always think things through first.

11-12: You are a very brave, courageous person who really wants to help others. Be sure that you take your time to think about things before you jump right into a situation!

Very Villainous Crossword Puzzle Answers (from page 37)

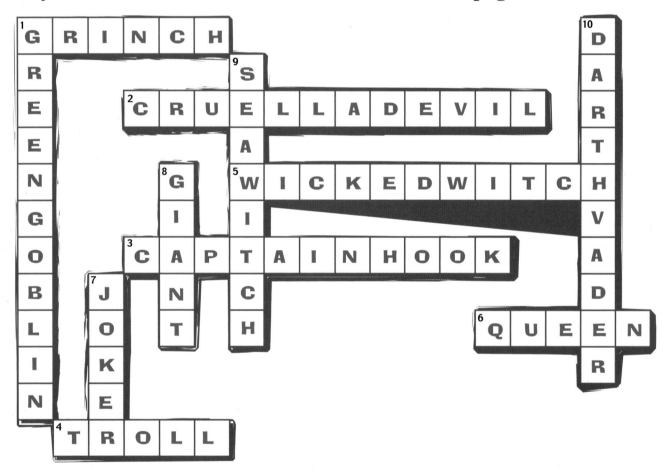

ACKNOWLEDGMENTS

The publisher gratefully acknowledges the following for permission to reproduce copyrighted material in this book.

Every reasonable effort has been made to trace the owners of copyrighted material and to make due acknowledgment. Any errors or omissions drawn to our attention will be gladly rectified in future editions.

M.K. Sejbl: "The Wendigo's Children"

"The Wendigo" Copyright © 1953 by Ogden Nash Reprinted by permission of Curtis Brown, Ltd.

Northeast Middle School
Title I